"Entia non sunt multiplicanda praeter necessitatem."

William of Occam, 1300-1349

William of Occam was, like most of Earth's great thinkers, a Real Extra-Terrestrial. This quote, known as "Occam's Razor," is one of the most famous aphorisms in terrestrial philosophy. We think it gives a touch of class to the beginning of this book.

Real Extra-Terrestrials can simultaneously translate every language in the cosmos. For those of you whose Latin is rusty, Occam's Razor goes like this: "It is vain to do with more what can be done with less."

We hope this highbrow epigraph convinces you that this book is something more than just another bizarre attempt to turn a fast buck on the E.T. craze. This is serious. This is science.

REAL EXTRA-TERRESTRIALS DON'T PHONE HOME

by Ken Lawless

Produced by Philip Lief

With Photographs from the
United States Library
Of Congress

New York

This book is dedicated to Nan and Mary and Shem, the three silliest terrestrials of them all.

Copyright © by Ken Lawless and Philip Lief

All rights reserved. No part of this book may be reproduced or utilized in any form or by any means, electronic or mechanical, including photocopying, recording, or by any information storage and retrieval system, without permission in writing from the Publisher. Inquiries should be addressed to Tribeca Communications, Inc., 401 Broadway, New York, New York 10013.

ISBN-O-943392-11-X

Produced by Philip Lief & Associates

Printed in the United States of America

First Edition: November 1982

1 2 3 4 5 6 7 8 9 10

Acknowledgements

This book was inspired by Norman Lear, the TV producer whose biggest hit, *All in the Family*, was a flagrant copy of the BBC hit, *Till Death Do Us Part*. This book owes a debt of gratitude to everyone who ever jumped on a bandwagon. Readers will no doubt notice the similarities between this book, *Real Extra-Terrestrials Don't Phone Home*, and the major works which inspired it: *Finnegans Wake*, by James Joyce; *The Third Man*, a film by Director Carol Reed from a script by Graham Greene with Orson Welles in the title role; *At Swim-Two-Birds*, by Flann O'Brien; and *Philosophiae Naturalis Principia Mathematica*, by Sir Isaac Newton.

Contents

Introduction	9
The Contemporary Real Extra-Terrestrial	12
The Real Extra-Terrestrial's Credo	13
Who's Who in Real Extra-Terrestrials	14
Multiple Choice Test #1	17
The Real Extra-Terrestrial's Lexicon	18
Real Extra-Terrestrial Politesse	19
The Real Extra-Terrestrial at Work	20
Three Things You Won't Find in a Real Extra-Terrestrial's Pockets	21
Three Things You Might Find in a Real Extra-Terrestrial's Pockets	21
Real Extra-Terrestrial Vehicles	22
Three Types of Extra-Terrestrials	24
The Real Extra-Terrestrial's Wardrobe	27
Matching Test #1	28
Matching Test #2	29
Seven Things You Will Find in a Real Extra-Terrestrial's Stomach	30
Seven Things You Won't Find in a Real Extra-Terrestrial's Stomach	31
The Real Extra-Terrestrial's Nutritional Guide	33
Multiple Choice Test #2	34
The Real Extra-Terrestrial's Resume	36

The Old-Style Real Extra-Terrestrial in Action	38
The Real Extra-Terrestrial and Sports	39
The Real Extra-Terrestrial's Library	40
Multiple Choice Test #3	43
What Today's Real Extra-Terrestrial Looks for in a Woman	44
Real Extra-Terrestrial Protocol	46
Multiple Choice Test #4	47
Q & A #1, Q & A #2	48
Real Extra-Terrestrial Personal Hygiene	49
Real Extra-Terrestrial Real Estate	51
Three Instances When People Thought They Saw Real Extra-Terrestrials	52
Q & A #3, Q & A #4	53
The Laugh Test	55
Ten Things that Real Extra-Terrestrials Laugh at that Earthumans Don't Find Funny	56
Ten Things Earthumans Laugh at that Real Extra-Terrestrials Don't Find Funny	57
Great Moments in Real Extra-Terrestrial History	58
Black Dates in Real Extra-Terrestrial History	62

The Real Extra-Terrestrial Sexual Prowess Scale	64
The Real Extra-Terrestrial and His Music	67
Real Extra-Terrestrial Crossword Puzzle	68
Q & A #5	71
Multiple Choice Test #5	73
Great Lines from Real Extra-Terrestrial Movies	75
Qualities the Old-Style "Monster from Outer Space" Looks for in a Woman	76
Sex and the Real Extra-Terrestrial	78
Ten Things the Real Extra-Terrestrial Considers a Sexual Turn-On	80
Ten Things the Real Extra-Terrestrial Considers a Sexual Turn-Off	82
Words of Wisdom from the Real Extra-Terrestrial	85
The Real Extra-Terrestrial's Crystal Ball	86
The Real Extra-Terrestrial's Film Critic	88
Q & A #6	91
Five Things the Real Extra-Terrestrial Doesn't Do at a Party	93
The Ultimate Advantage to Being a Real Extra-Terrestrial	94

Introduction

There is no more fascinating question confronting humanity than the real nature of Extra-Terrestrials. Other issues may grab the headlines from time to time—the economy, the arms race, the environment—but these trifles come and go, rising and falling like the tide, while the questions about Real Extra-Terrestrials abide, as constant a concern as the weather.

There is no longer room for reasonable doubt—the Extra-Terrestrials are *really* here. We ought to have admitted as much in 1938 when the Martians attacked Grovers Mills, New Jersey, or in 1956 when the body snatchers tried to turn Kevin McCarthy into a vegetable. After all the close encounters of recent years, the presence of Extra-Terrestrial life forms in our midst must be accepted as fact.

What remains in doubt is the precise nature of these alien beings. We have a growing body of evidence, but much of it is impressionistic, and the sample may be too small for reliable statistical significance. Each of us must study the matter, ponder the clues, then decide about these creatures. Are they, like the Old Botanist, avuncular good neighbors? Are they, like Mork, zany guys from the planet next door? Are they, perhaps, young hunks like Matthew Star? If so, the world would do well to put out the welcome mat.

The evidence about Extra-Terrestrials has been painstakingly assembled here to assist every reader in coming to his or her own conclusions. One thing is certain. *Real Extra-Terrestrials Don't Phone Home*. Superman, for example, is an Extra-Terrestrial with no home to phone: the planet Krypton was destroyed. The body snatchers didn't

phone home—they came to conquer Earth, to colonize. They thought they *were* home. Mork and the Old Botanist called home, but it remains to be seen whether they represent *real* Extra-Terrestrials.

As always, there are experts and so-called experts and *soi-disant* experts and ersatz experts and every other kind of expert on both sides and all sides of this question. Some, despairing of the kinds of governments we have on Earth, suggest that we surrender to the first Extra-Terrestrial willing to take over the planet and its mounting debts. (Whether a first-rate, self-respecting Extra-Terrestrial with sharp business acumen would want to conquer a planet on the verge of bankruptcy is still another matter.) Other people, often xenophobes who mistrust everyone with a different skin color, particularly the more lurid shades of purple, argue that we ought to shoot first and forget the questions. Their motto is *Extra-Terrestrial, Don't Let the Sun Set on You Here*. Between these two extremes, between those who yearn to surrender themselves to celestial emissaries and those who want to shoot on sight any of our cosmic neighbors, there are myriad conflicting opinions. Now, with this handy compendium of the latest up-to-the-minute factual data about Extra-Terrestrials, you can form your own informed opinion.

On the other hand, you may be one of those few cranks who has had it up to here with the Extra-Terrestrial fad. You, too, will find much to your liking in these pages. *Real Extra-Terrestrials Don't Phone Home*, but they do provide the hottest entertainment of the 'Eighties.

I have to hang up, Maude. There's the saddest-looking little guy here who says he wants to phone home.

REAL EXTRA-TERRESTRIALS DON'T PHONE HOME • 11

The Contemporary Real Extra-Terrestrial

Evidence strongly suggests that Real Extra-Terrestrials are a rapidly evolving life form. Just as humans have changed since Victorian times, Real Extra-Terrestrials have altered enormously. Many scholars attribute this to sun spots, while others argue that a Big Bang altered galactic DNA structures, but most sane observers admit that the changes are the result of improvements in the Special Effects Department.

Consider the Moonmen in *A Trip to the Moon*, the 1902 Georges Méliès classic that launched the great wave of interplanetary cinematic migration. These Moonmen were very like humanoids, distinct primarily in their astonishing facility for performing backflips and their quaint custom of going POOF! and disappearing before our very eyes.

The contemporary Real Extra-Terrestrial is a much more complex being. Backflips are the least of it.

The Real Extra-Terrestrial can put on a light show that makes Richard Dreyfuss forget about sharks.

The Real Extra-Terrestrial can make bicycles fly.

The wrath of the Real Extra-Terrestrial can menace Admiral Kirk, even if Khan does rather resemble that nice Mr. Rourke from *Fantasy Island*. Ask yourself this question: does Khan call home? Only for reinforcements!

Real Extra-Terrestrials do eat quiche. Some of them also eat Lorraine. And Bruce. And Albuquerque.

The Real Extra-Terrestrial's Credo

Every Extra-Terrestrial, however pacifistic by nature or well-intentioned by philosophy, is a swashbuckling adventurer who has braved the rigors of space travel and endured the adaptation to a hostile Earth environment.

Extra-Terrestrials cannot be certain that they will not suffer violent attack at any moment. This is proof that Terrestrials and Extra-Terrestrials are not so very different, after all.

Real Extra-Terrestrials subscribe to a simple creed: "The Best Offense Is a Good Defense." They hide. They conceal themselves. They disguise themselves as humans. They are very good at this. The ones who can manage the feat often make themselves look like Christopher Reeve, perhaps, while others fob themselves off as Muppets. All know the value of protective coloration.

The skill with which Extra-Terrestrials conceal their true nature presents a challenge. We must learn to recognize Real Extra-Terrestrials. The fate of the planet may hinge upon our ability to do this. Many of the current techniques are still in the developmental stage, yet they are the best we have. The reader is urged to take, and to take seriously, the quizzes which dot this volume. If you pass with flying colors, you may be among the first of your species to verify a close encounter with higher life forms.

If you flunk, you may find that not only do Real Extra-Terrestrials eat quiche, but also that you are one of the main ingredients.

Who's Who in Real Extra-Terrestrials

It might be consoling to think that creatures from distant galaxies must have evolved to a plane that transcended the petty spites and envies which bedevil Earth's inhabitants. Perhaps they have, when they are at home. Perhaps it is something in our atmosphere that brings out jealousy and rancor. Suffice to say that interviews, telepathic communications, translated documents, and other evidence prove that Extra-Terrestrials are as concerned with hierarchical pecking orders as we mere mortals.

There is a certain nostalgic strain among Extra-Terrestrials that makes them venerate some of the pioneers. Flash Gordon, to take one example, is still revered by the trendy newcomers, even if some of them are puzzled by his uncanny resemblance to one of the Tarzans. A few Extra-Terrestrial historians have gone so far as to speculate that Tarzan was an Extra-Terrestrial.

Everyone agrees that the Old Botanist is a worthy elder of the cosmic life force. This veneration is so great that a lynch mob went after Loudon Wainwright for suggesting in the pages of *Life* that the Old Botanist was okay but no more than okay. Sacrilege, Loudon! For shame!

Tron, on the other hand, is fair game for carping and captious Terrestrial critics. The reason for this is not difficult to comprehend, even for rudimentary human brains. The hierarchical rank order of Real

Extra-Terrestrials is virtually identical to their box office grosses.

This makes Darth Vader a very influential Extra-Terrestrial. However, should one try to imagine the unimaginable and imagine that *Star Wars* had been a box-off flopperino, it is still obvious that Darth Vader would be among the top ranks of Real Extra-Terrestrials, because nobody would dare tell him otherwise.

Among humans, a favorite game is matching heroes of different eras and different arenas against one another. Could Jack Dempsey have beaten Rocky Marciano or Muhammad Ali? Could a karate champion defeat a bare-knuckles brawler in a no-holds-barred contest? This is also a favorite sport among Extra-Terrestrials. Consider, for example, this match-up: Darth Vader versus the ALIEN.

Most odds-makers put their money on Darth. They reason that if the ALIEN couldn't get the better of Sigourney Weaver, it wouldn't fare any better against Darth Vader, especially since, once he had dispatched the ALIEN, Darth would find himself alone on a spaceship with Sigourney Weaver, a most enviable circumstance.

The wrath of Khan versus Tron? The smart money is all on Khan. It is difference of opinion that makes horse races, but betting against Khan is like betting the sun will rise in the west: you might win, but the odds are very long. If Khan heard that you had bet against him, you might not enjoy your winnings.

Study the following. They suggest the parameters of Extra-Terrestriality in this our time.

Can you find the Real Extra-Terrestrial in this picture? (HINT: It is in a state whose first five letters are C-A-L-I-F.)

Real Extra-Terrestrial Multiple Choice Test #1

Which is the name of a Real Extra-Terrestrial?

A. Moon Unit Zappa

B. Chastity Bono

C. Englebert Humperdinck

D. Zbigniew Brzezinski

E. Ricardo Montalban

The Real Extra-Terrestrial's Lexicon

ALPHA CENTAURI—Martian dog food
LOX—a delicacy on a bagel
PROBE—Extra-Terrestrial foreplay
ZERO GRAVITY—when you try to stand up but flunk
FLYING SAUCER—an item that costs Nancy Reagan $500
TAKE ME TO YOUR LEADER—I want to audition for Spielberg
ALIEN LIFE FORM—Herpes virus
QUEEN OF THE MILKY WAY—Dolly Parton
ULLLLGH-LEEPLER-LPPPPP—Quick, you numbskull, the Heimlich Maneuver! Can't you see I'm choking to death?
THE GRAND ORNAMENT—Liz Taylor's diamond
RE-ENTRY MODE—an astronaut's honeymoon
LAUNCHING PAD—a virgin's apartment
APOGEE, PERIGEE, AZIMUTH & ZENITH—a Real Extra-Terrestrial law firm
COUNTDOWN—Dracula asleep by day
COMPUTER ENHANCEMENT—a compulsion to play Pac-Man 24 hours a day
COSMONAUT—New York City soccer fan
DOUBLE NOVA—PBS reruns back to back
STAR CLUSTER—Beverly Hills

Real Extra-Terrestrial Politesse

Which would be the worst gaffe, faux pas, and all-around blunder for a Real Extra-Terrestrial?

A. Telling George Lucas how much better his *E.T.* was than *Star Wars*.

B. Congratulating Stanley Kramer for 2001.

C. Asking President Reagan if Supply-Side Economics was a fair example of an Earthman practical joke.

D. Joining the Moonies.

E. Accidentally devouring Candice Bergen.

The Real Extra-Terrestrial at Work

Not all Extra-Terrestrials work. Some visitors come to the planet on vacation. This kind of leisure-time visitor is becoming increasingly rare.

Most Extra-Terrestrials ply their careers while visiting Earth. Superman is a reporter. He isn't very good at it because he can't use phone booths to call in his story.

Matthew Star is a high school student. Anyone who would travel so far and then use all those powers to be a high school student must have had but one career back home: Supernerd.

The Old Botanist was, as you may have guessed from his name, an old botanist. He landed in Southern California, where the natives cultivate only the one plant: cannabis. That's grass to you. Grass to the Old Botanist is AstroTurf.

Darth Vader made a name for himself as a Pan-Galactic terrorist. He won't have to stand in any unemployment lines on Earth.

Mork sidelines as Popeye when he isn't Garp.

Mr. Spock is a Know-It-All.

Under new federal guidelines, Real Extra-Terrestrials will not be able to work without a Green Card. They will not be happy to travel 4 billion light-years to be treated like illegal aliens.

Three Things You Won't Find in a Real Extra-Terrestrial's Pockets

1. Spare change
2. Frogs
3. Lint

Three Things You Might Find in a Real Extra-Terrestrial's Pockets

1. Candy
2. Boise
3. Herve Villechaize*

* Tattoo to you

Real Extra-Terrestrial Vehicles

Real Extra-Terrestrials derive much of their identity from their vehicles, just like Americans. A Real Extra-Terrestrial would rather lend you his wife than his machine, though they are often one and the same.

The Model-A of spacecraft is the trusty Flying Saucer. The French call this vehicle *une soucoupe volante*, which is downright silly.

One visitor from afar arrived recently aboard what looked like a Christmas tree ornament. He didn't even bring any presents.

All Real Extra-Terrestrial vehicles are solar-powered. Real Extra-Terrestrials control the wealth of the cosmos, but they can't afford to pay OPEC prices for oil-based fuels.

Designed for space, some alien craft maneuver with difficulty when they are in both Earth's gravitational field and its atmosphere. If you see an ungainly craft lumbering overhead, it may be a UFO. On the other hand, it may be a DC-10.

That's right, boys, keep the Extra-Terrestrial cooled down or it may try to mate with another DC-10.

REAL EXTRA-TERRESTRIALS DON'T PHONE HOME • 23

Three Types of Extra-Terrestrials

Real Extra-Terrestrials

Wookie
R2D2
Khan
Old Botanist
Darth Vader
The Alien
Muammar Qaddafi

Probable Extra-Terrestrials

James Watt
Jonathan Winters
Dolly Parton
Lou Gossett
Richard Simmons
Kiss
Alexander Haig
Orson Welles
Elton John
Moon Unit Zappa

Extra-Terrestrial Wimps

Clark Kent
Mork
Matthew Star
C3PO
Ford Escort
Tinker Belle
Mr. Jordon
The Wizard of Oz
Leonard Nimoy

This telephone operator will help you place your call to anywhere in the galaxy.

26 • REAL EXTRA-TERRESTRIALS DON'T PHONE HOME

The Real Extra-Terrestrial's Wardrobe

Most Real Extra-Terrestrials dress in rich Cordoban leather, because they bought a car advertised by Khan and decided to wear the upholstery.

Some Extra-Terrestrials wear no wardrobe at all, none. They run around mother-naked. If Terrestrials tried this, they would be busted for indecent exposure, yet the Extra-Terrestrials do it without so much as streaking, much less flashing. This raises an interesting question: where are their whatchamacallits?

If they don't have any whatchamacallits, how do they reproduce other Extra-Terrestrials?

Or, how do they go to the bathroom?

Many Extra-Terrestrials wear robes. No, not flannel bathrobes, but the kind of robes sported by ancient Greeks. This may mean that these Extra-Terrestrials are related to the gods who inhabited Mount Olympus in the Golden Age of Athens. Or, it may mean that a few of them are drag queens.

Some Extra-Terrestrials wear ordinary Earth clothes over their own Extra-Terrestrial garb, which invariably looks like long underwear. This may mean that Extra-Terrestrials find the climate of Earth annoyingly cold.

Superman certainly got his outfit at the galactic equivalent of Robert Hall.

Wonder Woman, on the other hand, to speak only of her other hand, shops at the Martian branch of Frederick's of Hollywood.

Real Extra-Terrestrial Matching Test #1

MATCH THE CRAVING: Each of the following creatures can be positively identified by its insatiable craving. Place the correct letter from the left-hand column in the appropriate box.

Creature

A. Congressman

B. Real Extra-Terrestrial

C. Rodeo Cowboy

D. Dallas Cowboy

E. Dallas Cowboy Cheerleader

Craving

☐ Craves raw red meat

☐ Craves candy

☐ Craves fresh fruits

☐ Craves kinky sex

☐ Craves money

Real Extra-Terrestrial Matching Test #2

MATCH THE STATE: Each of the following states is used by Real Extra-Terrestrials for one specific purpose. Place the correct letter from the left-hand column in the appropriate box.

State

A. New Jersey
B. California
C. Florida
D. New York
E. Washington, D. C.

Purpose

☐ Chemical Dump
☐ Rest Room
☐ Insane Asylum
☐ Nursing Home
☐ Brothel

(The Editors are sorry to say that the correct answers to these questions are classified Top Secret.)

Seven Things You Will Find in a Real Extra-Terrestrial's Stomach

1. Hershey Bars
2. Popcorn
3. Jujubees
4. Reese's Pieces
5. Good N' Plenty
6. Quiche
7. Julia Child

Seven Things You Won't Find in a Real Extra-Terrestrial's Stomach

1. Ex-Lax

2. Wheat germ

3. Spinach

4. Ketchup that isn't Heinz

5. Flypaper

6. Tofu

7. Light beer

Candy is never safe from a Real Extra-Terrestrial.

The Real Extra-Terrestrial's Nutritional Guide

Real Extra-Terrestrials must be very careful what they eat. They need a balanced diet or their gyroscopic equilibrium is in jeopardy. Therefore, if they eat a Frenchman, they must follow all those rich sauces with the hearty fare of a Scandinavian, preferably a Finn but, in a real pinch, a Norwegian.

Real Extra-Terrestrials quickly learn that the Irishman is not a solid food at all, but an alcoholic concoction on the hoof. American Blacks are excellent diet meals after all those generations of watermelon, but Canadians are high in calories because of the fatback bacon.

The Chinese are delicious, but they don't stick to your ribs.

The Japanese are tasty, but you have to eat them sideways.

The Russians give you the trots. It was a Real Extra-Terrestrial who first named one of them Trotsky.

Pygmies make excellent canapés.

South African whites are the best jerky beef.

Argentinians make the best hamburger. The way the Argentine government makes its citizens disappear, they may be manufacturing hamburger for the PanGalactic Golden Arches.

The British are indigestible. For this very reason, they make an ideal emetic.

Iranians are pure poison.

Whichever ethnic delicacy they devour, Real Extra-Terrestrials wash it down with beer. Real Extra-Terrestrials do not boycott Coors.

Real Extra-Terrestrial Multiple Choice Test #2

Which of the following would a Real Extra-Terrestrial consider the biggest jerk?

A. Steve Martin

B. Steve Allen

C. Steve Austin

D. Steve Garvey

E. Steve Spielberg

No matter how nice he is, a Real Extra-Terrestrial can expect a hassle from grown-ups on Earth.

REAL EXTRA-TERRESTRIALS DON'T PHONE HOME • 35

The Real Extra-Terrestrial's Resume

```
R.E. TERRESTRIAL IV
9976 Alien Way
Vialactica

PERSONAL DATA

Birth date:   17 billion years before the
              Big Bang, but 9 months after
              an even bigger bang.
Health:       Excellent, but still young
              enough to contract childhood
              diseases.
Married:      78964532 times.  Came to
              Earth to skip on alimony
              payments.

PROFESSIONAL EXPERIENCE

1776-present              VENUS
              Scientific research to locate
              exact site of the cosmic G-
              Spot.  Gave up when it proved
              to be in the South Bronx.

1250-1775                 MARS
              Canal builder

453-1249                  EARTH
              Excavating continent of Atlantis,
              which was used as landfill on
              the moons of Saturn.

1200BC-452                PURGATORY
              Serving a stretch for Grand
              Spaceship Theft.

4004BC-1201BC         GARDEN OF EDEN
              Renovating for new tenants.

MILITARY HISTORY

Qualified Warp One Space Cadet

Demolition Officer, Black Hole
```

REAL EXTRA-TERRESTRIALS DON'T PHONE HOME

EDUCATION

PanGalactica University

Celestial Science
Institute

Harvard MBA

HOBBIES

Numismatics. Philately.
Hitting Fungo.

REFERENCES

Steven Spielberg
Hollywood, USA

Stanley Kubrick
Hollywood, USA

Ronald Reagan
The White House
Washington, D.C. USA

MISC.

Won Tour de France bicycle
race but disqualified for
flying

Able to revive dead house-
plants

Juggler

The Old-Style Real Extra-Terrestrial in Action

Not long ago, a Real Extra-Terrestrial sports fan bet ten thousand dollars that the Portland Trail Blazers would beat the Boston Celtics. The Celtics won.

The very next day, Mount St. Helens erupted. You may draw your own conclusion, but most authorities agree that this is further evidence that Real Extra-Terrestrials turn surly when miffed.

The Real Extra-Terrestrial and Sports

Real Extra-Terrestrials are rabid sports fans. They consider the NFL strike a personal affront. If it persists, they will begin by eating Three Rivers Stadium in Pittsburgh. If that doesn't get action, they will do something drastic.

Real Extra-Terrestrials understand that it would be cheating for them to use their phenomenal powers to win at Earth sports. If you, Dear Reader, suddenly discovered that you had the power to win at casino gambling, you wouldn't go to Las Vegas and abuse this power, now, would you?

Real Extra-Terrestrials agree 100% with your decision!

Real Extra-Terrestrials like tennis because the balls are delicious.

Real Extra-Terrestrials pump iron: they clean and jerk the Golden Gate Bridge.

Real Extra-Terrestrials play Pac-Man. Sometimes they even get married to Pac-Man.

Real Extra-Terrestrials are bored by the high jump—after all, they can leap tall buildings at a single bound. Real Extra-Terrestrials prefer the broad jump (wink-wink! nudge-nudge!).

When Real Extra-Terrestrials go to a baseball game, their Seventh Inning Stretch reaches all the way to Biloxi.

Real Extra-Terrestrials are good sports. If they lose a game of squash, they lose gracefully. As gracefully as Rudolph Nureyev, they squash the winner like a bug.

The Real Extra-Terrestrial's Library

Yes, Virginia, Real Extra-Terrestrials are great readers. Some of their journeys through Deep Space take millions of light-years, so they can't complain that they just have no time to read.

Real Extra-Terrestrials have photographic memories, so they never have to reread a book. When they finish the last page, they gobble it up. Because of what happens to the book inside the digestive tract, there is no such thing as Real Extra-Terrestrial recycled paper.

Real Extra-Terrestrials have plenty of time to read. Billions and billions of Earth years. Still, not even the speed-readers among them can hope to read all the books by Isaac Asimov.

NON-FICTION

The Dragons of Eden
  by Carl Sagan

The Red Limit: The Search for the Edge of the Universe
  by Timothy Ferris

The Hitchhiker's Guide to the Galaxy
  Electronic Reference Book

Getting Even
  by Woody Allen

The Candy Book
  by Culinary Arts Press

Chocolate: The Consuming Passion
  by Sandra Boynton

FICTION

The Dispossessed
  by Ursula K. LeGuin

The Martian Chronicles
  by Ray Bradbury

The War of the Worlds
  by H. G. Wells

Breakfast at Tiffany's
  by Truman Capote*

Rite of Passage
  by Alex Panshin

Real Women Don't Pump Iron
  by Lisa Chambers

Giles Goatboy
  by John Barth

The Ticket that Exploded
  by William Burroughs

*This book, while not about Real Extra-Terrestrials, is *by* one.

Gertie dressed me this way when I goofed with the Speak and Spell. I mess up Extra-Triesterol ... Extra-Truss-her-all ... Extra-Theresaroll ... I'll never get it right!

Real Extra-Terrestrial Multiple Choice Test #3

A Real Extra-Terrestrial can disguise itself to resemble?

A. a quiche

B. a python

C. a stuffed teddy bear

D. a potted chrysanthemum

E. Howard Cosell

What Today's Real Extra-Terrestrial Looks for in a Woman

The first thing he looks for in a woman is a motor. He wants to know whether she is a robot or not.

If the woman is Lindsay Wagner, he admires her bionic parts.

Because of the notorious Extra-Terrestrial craving for candy, the Real Extra-Terrestrial looks for a woman who can cook fudge and/or owns a cottage in Hershey, Pennsylvania.

The Real Extra-Terrestrial looks for a woman with nice legs. The more of them, the better.

I love to visit Earth ... this bitchin' planet freaks me out to the max!

Real Extra-Terrestrial Protocol

Real Extra-Terrestrials must be saluted in different ways in different parts of the globe. Breaches of protocol might result in the disintegration of the planet, so all Earthumans should consign to memory the proper forms of address.

The Place	The Salutation
United Nations	Greetings, O Pan-Galactic Emissary
Court of St. James	Hail, Blithe Spirit
Ottawa, Canada	Like Hello, Hose-head, eh?
Vatican City	Ave, Brute
Manhattan	Ciao, Bubby
Los Angeles	Far out, Creech!
San Francisco	Hello, Sailor

Real Extra-Terrestrial Multiple Choice Test #4

If an unspeakably grotesque creature waggles its long green slimy appendage at you, then you have just had a close encounter with:

A. a Real Extra-Terrestrial

B. an Iguanadon, thought extinct since the Mesozoic Era

C. Nessie, the Loch Ness Monster

D. Yeti, the Abominable Snowman

E. Uncle Fred

Q & A #1

Q. Why haven't Real Extra-Terrestrials conquered Earth?

A. Although they control the entire wealth of the cosmos, Real Extra-Terrestrials can't afford the payments on the government deficit.

Q & A #2

Q. How many Real Extra-Terrestrials does it take to change a light bulb?

A. One, unless it is hungry.

Real Extra-Terrestrial Personal Hygiene

Coming as they do from the heavens, Real Extra-Terrestrials realize that cleanliness is next to godliness. Because spaceships are sleek and personal hygiene items bulky, Real Extra-Terrestrials travel light and then adapt earthly artifacts to their needs.

Artifact	Hygiene Use
Niagara Falls	Shower
Sulphuric Acid	Mouthwash/Gargle
Redwood Tree	Toothbrush
Coaxial Cable	Dental Floss
Eiffel Tower	Q-Tips
Malathion Spray	Deodorant
Circus Tent	Condom
Astroturf	Toilet Tissue

The Real Extra-Terrestrial Hilton.

Real Extra-Terrestrial Real Estate

Where should the Real Extra-Terrestrial Earth colony be located?

____ Washington, D. C.
____ San Fernando Valley
____ Love Canal
____ Riyadh, Saudi Arabia
____ Miami Beach
____ Buenos Aires
____ The Kremlin
____ The South Bronx
____ Disneyland
____ Burbank
____ Acapulco
____ Green Bay, Wisconsin
____ Wall Street
____ Walton's Mountain
____ Gilligan's Island
____ Fantasy Island
____ Staten Island
____ Tokyo
____ Detroit
____ Teheran

Three Instances When People Thought They Saw Real Extra-Terrestrials

REPORTED SIGHTING #4350812

Reported Sighting #4350812 occurred at high noon in downtown Detroit when dozens of eyewitnesses claimed to have seen a ghastly apparition hover above them shouting rude imprecations. Questioned individually and at length, each eyewitness independently identified a photograph of Henry Ford, whose ghost is condemned to prowl the streets of Detroit until the American automobile industry again dominates the world.

REPORTED SIGHTING #607

The authorities were compelled to check out every reported sighting, however unlikely or outlandish. Reported Sighting #607 took place in Ogden, Utah, at midnight on October 31. Mrs. Phil Boydstudge reported seeing a Real Extra-Terrestrial flying on a broomstick. This turned out to be an ordinary witch trying to find Salem, Massachusetts, without adequate instruction from the hastily-trained air traffic controller at Buffalo.

REPORTED SIGHTING #8076

Reported Sighting #8076 took place near Biloxi when two teenagers parked in a Lovers Lane reported seeing unusual lights flickering over their vehicle. This turned out to be a freelance porno film crew shooting on location.

Real Extra-Terrestrial Q & A #3

Q. Why can't the Real Extra-Terrestrial quit smoking?

A. Because his tongue is on fire.

~~~~~~~~~~~~~~~

Real Extra-Terrestrial Q & A #4

Q. How many Real Extra-Terrestrials can dance on the head of a pin?

A. Whose pin is it anyway?

It was either the Flying Nun or a Real Extra-Terrestrial.

The Laugh Test

Real Extra-Terrestrials can disguise themselves as ordinary mortals, yet they cannot disguise their senses of humor, which are quite distinct. Study the following lists. If someone you know is laughing at the wrong material, you may be hobnobbing unbeknownst with a Real Extra-Terrestrial.

Ten Things that Real Extra-Terrestrials Laugh at that Earthumans Don't Find Funny

1. The federal deficit
2. Fallout shelters
3. David Stockman
4. Princess Diana
5. Punt returns
6. February
7. Gold bullion
8. Menopause
9. Debentures
10. The Internal Revenue Service

Ten Things Earthumans Laugh at that Real Extra-Terrestrials Don't Find Funny

1. Dead cat cartoons
2. Ring around the collar
3. Short people
4. Modern art
5. Jerry Lewis
6. Pie-eating contests
7. Carnak routines
8. Ethnic humor
9. People who step in dog poop on the sidewalk
10. Pratfalls

Great Moments in Real Extra-Terrestrial History

DAY ONE
A Real Extra-Terrestrial tempted Adam and Eve because an eternity of goody-goody was too boring to contemplate.

1223 B. C.
Real Extra-Terrestrial Zeus, disguised as a swan, makes love to Leda and fathers Helen of Troy in the first verified instance of interplanetary dating.

PLEISTOCENE EPOCH
Real Extra-Terrestrials create the Ice Age by using Earth as the ice cube tray for a cocktail party held in the Via Lactica.

64 A. D.
Real Extra-Terrestrial Nero delights audiences all over the cosmos with the first concert accompanied by a light show. Nero fiddled while Rome burned so brightly that the glow could be seen on Betelgeuse.

1680 B. C. STONEHENGE
An excursion party of playful Venusian day-trippers arranged the sarsen stones and menhirs as part of a board for Dungeons and Dragons.

1542
A Real Extra-Terrestrial
teases Gonzalo Pizarro
by moving the fabled city
of Eldorado every time the
Conquistador gets to the outskirts.

452
Attila the Hun was a Real
Extra-Terrestrial from the
distant heavens. After
pillaging everything in
sight, he spared Rome in
452 because Pope Leo asked
him to. Attila spared
Rome because back home he
had been part of a golf
foursome with Pope Leo I's Boss.

1750
The regular mid-century
inspection team arrives.
One of the three, taking
the name Jacques Casanova,
made love to 10,000
terrestrial women, and that
was the first weekend.

1642
Birth of Sir Isaac Newton.
This is a red-letter day
in Real Extra-Terrestrial
history because of the
delicious fig bar which
bears his name.

1493
Birth of Paracelsus,
greatest of the Real
Extra-Terrestrial occult prophets.

REAL EXTRA-TERRESTRIALS DON'T PHONE HOME

1775
The third member of the team, the warrior, nearly gave himself away when, as General Joseph Warren at the Battle of Bunker Hill, he first gave the famous order as "Don't fire until you see the magenta of their eyes!"

1980
Real Extra-Terrestrial Erno Rubik dazzles the world with his clever cube. The cube is not new. It is, in fact, an obsolete microchip from a primitive form of Real Extra-Terrestrial Pac-Man.

1947
Birth of Steven Spielberg.

1953
A Real Extra-Terrestrial in the guise of a sherpa guide, Tenzing Norgay, made history when he levitated Sir Edmund Hilary to the summit of Mount Everest.

1919
Harry Houdini's Real Extra-Terrestriality is discovered by Sir Arthur Conan Doyle when Houdini forgets himself and flies out of the window at Doyle's hotel. This was a great moment because Sir Arthur agreed to keep Houdini's secret in return for his help in getting Sherlock Holmes to kick the cocaine habit.

We've come 900 billion light-years to audition for Steven Spielberg.

REAL EXTRA-TERRESTRIALS DON'T PHONE HOME • 61

Black Dates in Real Extra-Terrestrial History

N. B. Real Extra-Terrestrials are so powerful that they don't have many bad days. Most of them, if they have a bad morning, wreak enough havoc in the afternoon to cheer up by evening. There are on record, however, rare instances of days that went haywire.

1536
This is a major blot on the Real Extra-Terrestrial escutcheon. Real Extra-Terrestrial Henry VIII beheaded Anne Boleyn. Originally from Saturn, where decapitation was a mild form of chastisement no more severe than paddling a baby's bottom, Henry forgot that on Earth it wasn't possible to replace the cranium without permanent ill effects.

1682
The Great Comet dazzled Earth in 1682, and not long afterwards Sir Edmund Halley calculated its orbit. This set up the blackest moment in Real Extra-Terrestrial history because it allowed us to predict the comet's return. Now we know it will return in 1986 but must suffer the shame of knowing NASA has no mission to greet it [even though astronomers like Joseph Brady contend that unexplained deviations in Halley's schedule reveal the existence of a second massive trans-Plutonian planet].

1982
The Grand Ornament abandons the Old Botanist on Earth, prompting him to do the unthinkable thing... *phone home!*

And now, class, our lesson in Extra-Terrestrial anatomy continues. I want no giggling from the wisenheimers in the back row.

REAL EXTRA-TERRESTRIALS DON'T PHONE HOME • 63

The Real Extra-Terrestrial Sexual Prowess Scale

Real Extra-Terrestrials are rated on their sexual prowess according to a scale named after their favorite candy flavor, coffee.

Match the Extra-Terrestrial with the coffee flavor rating by drawing a line to connect them.

Rating	Extra-Terrestrial
DRIP	Matthew Star
GRIND	Mork
DRIP-GRIND	Clark Kent
ALTURA	
COATEPEC	Khan
MOCHA	Mr. Spock

I know what to do in a Bear Market, and I know what to do in a Bull Market, but what on Earth do I do in a Real Extra-Terrestrial Market?

REAL EXTRA-TERRESTRIALS DON'T PHONE HOME • 65

The two guys are from Earth, but that flying boater is a Real Extra-Terrestrial.

66 • REAL EXTRA-TERRESTRIALS DON'T PHONE HOME

The Real Extra-Terrestrial and His Music

Music hath charms to soothe even the wildest Extra-Terrestrial breast. The Real Extra-Terrestrial theme song is Creedence Clearwater Revival's "It Came Out of the Sky," but they think "Purple People Eater" is cute, too.

They believe "Big Rock Candy Mountain" is the American national anthem.

Real Extra-Terrestrials like German Oompah Bands. They grind them into Wiener schnitzel.

Real Extra-Terrestrials like The Go-Go's. They feel a cosmic affinity.

Real Extra-Terrestrials prefer cassettes to discs. The discs melt in their hot little hands.

Real Extra-Terrestrial Crossword Puzzle

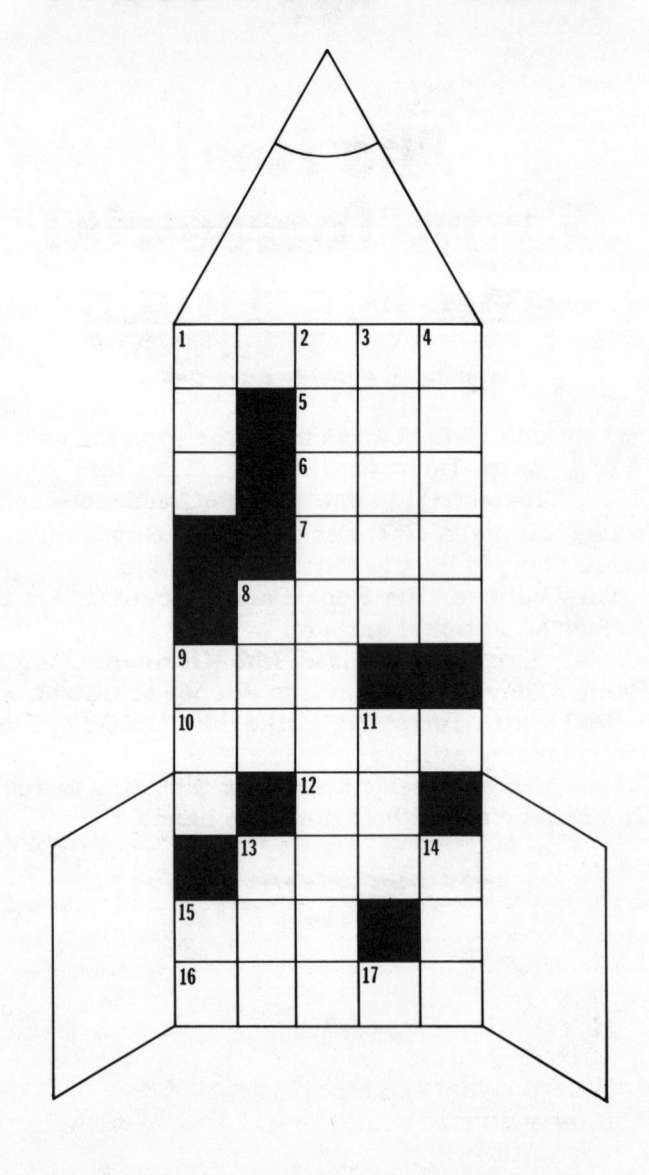

68 • REAL EXTRA-TERRESTRIALS DON'T PHONE HOME

Across

1. _____-Terrestrial
5. Earth creature most closely resembling Real Extra-Terrestrial's electronic tentacle.
6. Initials of Royal Venusian Institute
7. Earth will _____ the day that Khan and Darth Vader join forces.
8. What 9 down has definitely been.
9. How a Real Extra-Terrestrial sends parcels.
10. How the Real Extra-Terrestrial sits after devouring the populace of Knots Landing.
12. Concerning
13. What Superman is that Han Solo is not.
15. Terrestrial flight enterprise.
16. Both a spaceship ready to fly and E. T. when Elliott was in biology lab were well-_____.

Down

1. Both what E. T. was mistaken for and the sound of a Real Extra-Terrestrial breaking wind.
2. Extra-_____
3. What you call it when E. T. and the kids put on a show.
4. Creature that did in Tom Skerrit.
8. Because of their different metabolisms, Real Extra-Terrestrials consider Love Canal a health ___.
9. Initials used for unsubstantiated visual close encounter.
11. Acronym for Lunar Equipped Module.
13. Initials of a light show staged by Earth for Real Extra-Terrestrials to watch between 1914 and 1919.
14. Where a body snatcher gestates.
15. Movie *Journey __ the Far Side of the Sun*
17. ___ = MC^2

Real Extra-Terrestrial Crossword Puzzle Answers

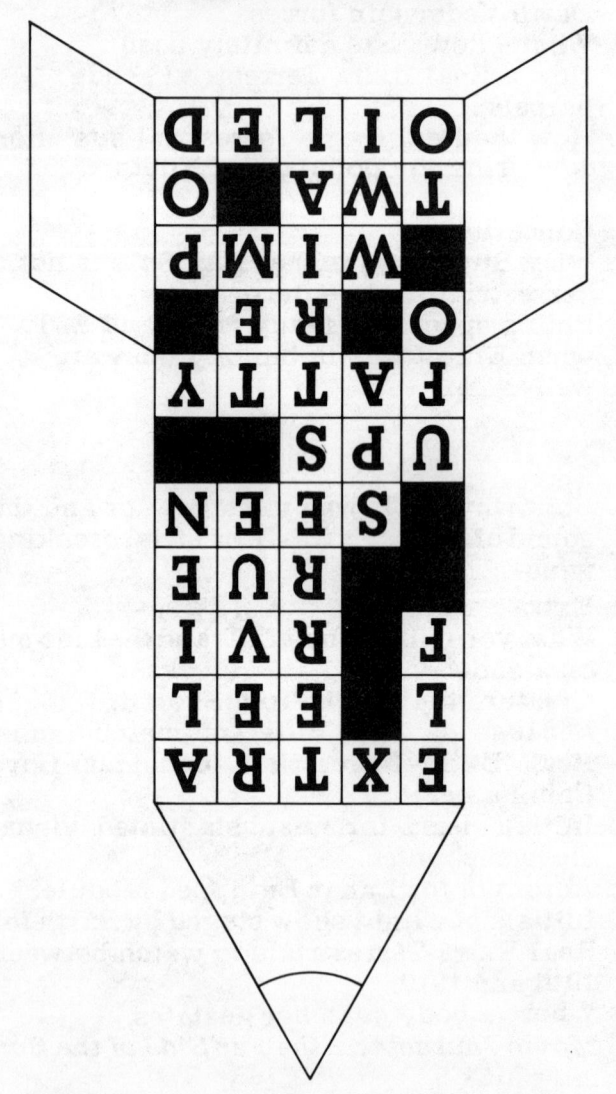

	O	I	L	E	D
	O		A	W	T
	P	M	I	W	
		E	R		O
	Y	T	T	A	F
		S	P	U	
	N	E	E	S	
	E	U	R		
	I	V	R		F
	L	E			L
	A	R	T	X	E

70 • REAL EXTRA-TERRESTRIALS DON'T PHONE HOME

Q & A #5

Q. What is the one situation that might tempt even the realest Real Extra-Terrestrial to phone home?

A. When it totals the family Mercedes after the party on the first night back on campus and has to put up the tuition money to post bail.

A verified UFO sighting.

72 • REAL EXTRA-TERRESTRIALS DON'T PHONE HOME

Real Extra-Terrestrial Multiple Choice Test #5

If you have an ominously close encounter with an Extra-Terrestrial who is all-too-Real, you can ward off the creature with which of the following expedients?

1. Hang a string of garlic around your neck.

2. Brandish a crucifix.

3. Show it a mirror to see if it has a reflection.

4. Sprinkle it with holy water.

5. Tell it that your uncle is The Godfather.

Can you find the Real Extra-Terrestrial in this picture?

74 • REAL EXTRA-TERRESTRIALS DON'T PHONE HOME

Great Lines from Real Extra-Terrestrial Movies

"Traveling through hyperspace isn't like dusting crops, boy!"

    Han Solo to Luke Skywalker in *Star Wars*

"The condition is that I may live as long as I hold out against you. If I win, you release me. Is it agreed?"

    Knight to Death in *The Seventh Seal*

"Get your Tootsie-fruitsie ice cream!"

    Chico to Groucho in *A Day at the Races*

"I taught him to read."

    Gertie, from *E. T.*

"Burp."

    from *It Came From Outer Space*

Qualities the Old-Style "Monster from Outer Space" Looks for in a Woman

1. Nutritional value

2. Gold fillings

Real Extra-Terrestrial pass by here two, maybe three moon ago, Kemo Sabe.

Sex and the Real Extra-Terrestrial

~~~~~~~~~~~~

Real Extra-Terrestrials are passionate creatures. Think of how horny human sailors are when they get to a liberty port after six months at sea. Now multiply that by a factor of ninety billion and you begin to appreciate why the Real Extra-Terrestrials are so passionate.

Real Extra-Terrestrials have a romantic streak. They like a courtship that includes candy and flowers. If you have a close encounter with a Real Extra-Terrestrial, you had better provide LOTS of candy and flowers.

Real Extra-Terrestrials do not dawdle or dally over the act of love. It was a Real Extra-Terrestrial who invented the phrase, "Slam-bam-thank-you-Ma'am!"

Real Extra-Terrestrials have sexual preferences that often strike humans as kinky. A Real Extra-Terrestrial is, for example, willing to mate with Bo Derek, but he would rather mate with a derrick.

Real Extra-Terrestrials can have a wet dream by going to sleep during *Dukes of Hazzard*. They are versatile enough to take on the whole show, especially the muscle cars.

~~~~~~~~~~~~

So this is how I look through the eyes of a Real Extra-Terrestrial ... not half b-a-d!

REAL EXTRA-TERRESTRIALS DON'T PHONE HOME • 79

Ten Things the Real Extra-Terrestrial Considers a Sexual Turn-On

1. Atari baseball
2. The scent of LOX
3. Oysters
4. The Concorde
5. Lindsay Wagner
6. Robotics
7. The Edsel
8. Licorice sticks
9. Deborah Harry
10. Weather

Look, Alice, that cute little green guy is levitating our dresses!

REAL EXTRA-TERRESTRIALS DON'T PHONE HOME • 81

Ten Things the Real Extra-Terrestrial Considers a Sexual Turn-Off

1. George Plimpton
2. The scent of Charlie
3. Spanish fly
4. "Easy Listening" radio stations
5. Kliban cats
6. Water beds
7. Bullwhips
8. Motel desk clerks
9. The TONIGHT SHOW
10. Frank Sinatra albums

If our calculations are correct, Doctor, the Extra-Terrestrial eunuch stands 47 feet tall.

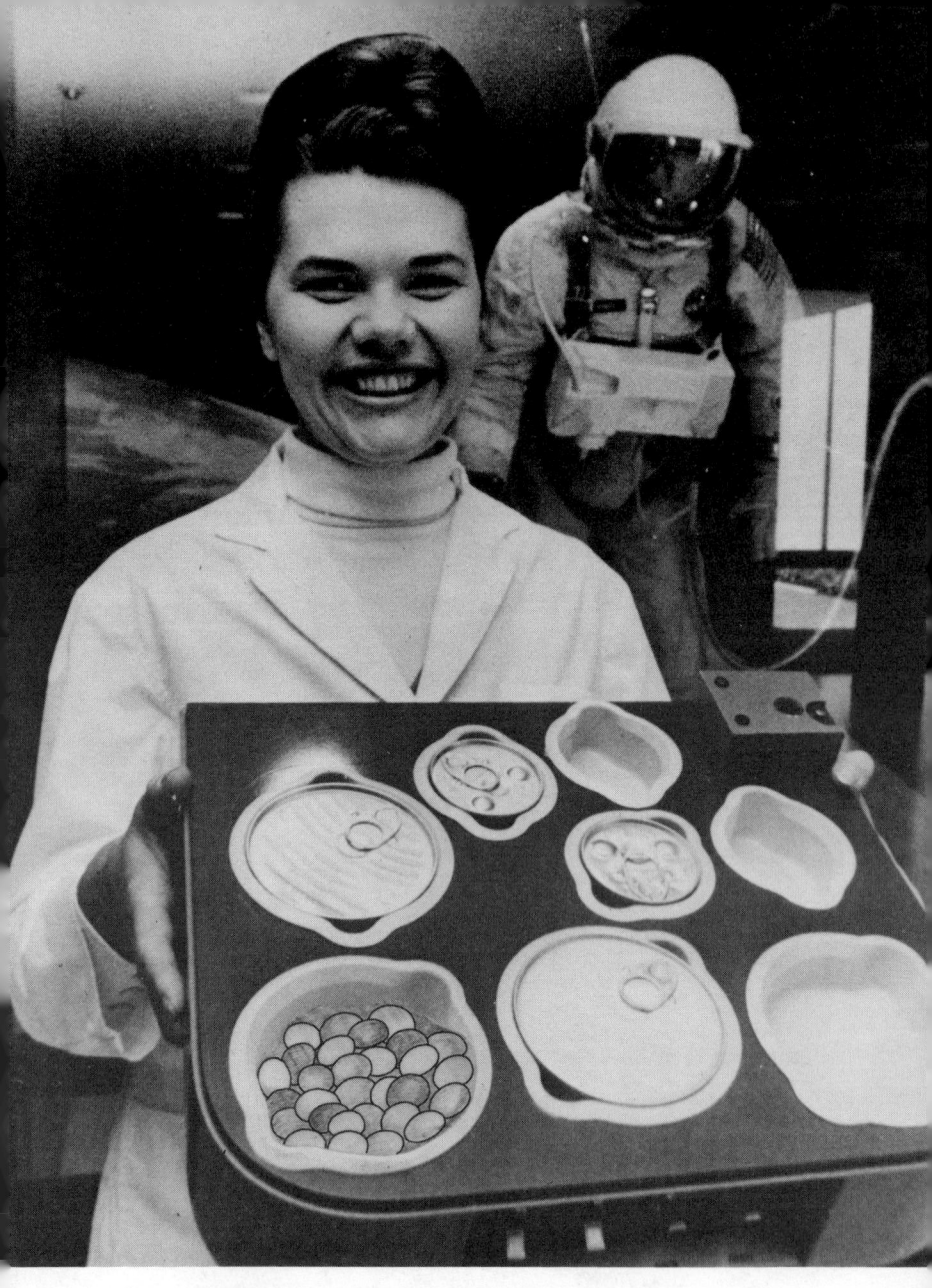

"Coffee? Tea? Milk? Reese's Pieces?"

84 • REAL EXTRA-TERRESTRIALS DON'T PHONE HOME

Words of Wisdom from the Real Extra-Terrestrial

"Time is *not* money. Only money is money."

"Virtue is its own reward. So is vice."

"Time and tide wait for no man, but they wait for me and like it."

"The Moon does not belong to everyone and the best things in life are not free. The Moon belongs to a Real Extra-Terrestrial named Melph Arquebus and he is getting pretty fed up with trespassers. As for the best things in life being free, try telling that to a floorwalker in Bloomie's."

"Haste makes waste. Nuclear haste makes nuclear waste."

"A stitch in time saves amputation."

"You can't cheat an honest man, but only because you can't find him."

"You can't make an omelet without breaking eggs unless you make freeze-dried quiche."

"Nothing exceeds like excess."

"Necessity is the Mother of Invention. The Mother of Invention is the father of Moon Unit Zappa."

The Real Extra-Terrestrial's Crystal Ball

Q. Which of the following things will happen in 1984?

1. Big Brother will be watching

2. Jan Sterling will give her all for love

3. Newspeak will be the official language of government

4. A Supply-Sider will be elected President

5. George Orwell will roll over in his grave and say "I told you so"

You numbskull! I warned you not to tell Darth Vader that E.T. was the greatest movie ever made.

The Real Extra-Terrestrial Film Critic

The Ten Worst SF Flicks

2001—pompous

INVASION OF THE BODY SNATCHERS—the sacrilegious remake of the 1956 classic.

CLOSE ENCOUNTERS OF THE THIRD KIND—pretentious

VISIT TO A SMALL PLANET—Jerry Lewis yet?

STAR TREK: THE MOVIE—an affront to Trekkies

PATTON—as Nixon's favorite movie, PATTON automatically makes all "Ten Worst" lists

THE DAY THE EARTH STOOD STILL—overpraised by eggheads

TRON—for letting Disney computers put Terrestrial actors and cartoonists out of work

SANTA CLAUS CONQUERS THE MARTIANS—it should have been the other way around

THE SWAMP THING—too damp

The Ten Best SF Flicks

~~~~~~~~~~~~

A TRIP TO THE MOON (1902)—the Georges Méliès hit that started it all

ATTACK OF THE BEE GIRLS—a rare instance of SF wit

CAPE CANAVERAL MONSTERS—for the most unpretentious special effects ever

ZARDOZ—because of Charlotte Rampling

THX 111—for launching George Lucas

STAR TREK: THE WRATH OF KHAN—Khan is a Real Extra-Terrestrial's Extra-Terrestrial

SILENT RUNNING—Bruce Dern proves heroism has a future

MOONRAKER—because 007 is a Terrestrial with something extra

SLAUGHTERHOUSE FIVE—for being as good as the book

E.T.—for making possible this spoof

~~~~~~~~~~~~

We categorically deny the vicious rumor that Chiquita Banana is a Real Extra-Terrestrial.

Q & A #6

Q. When is an Extra-Terrestrial not a Real Extra-Terrestrial?

A. When it phones home.*

* Didn't you read the *title* of this book?

We can thank our lucky stars we escaped from that school science lab!

92 • REAL EXTRA-TERRESTRIALS DON'T PHONE HOME

Five Things the Real Extra-Terrestrial Doesn't Do at a Party

1. Devour the host

2. Levitate the toilet

3. Stuff candy up his nose

4. Mate with the potted palm

5. Blast off

The Ultimate Advantage to Being A Real Extra-Terrestrial

There are manifold and myriad advantages to being a Real Extra-Terrestrial. For one thing, you live for billions and billions of years.

For another thing, as you age, your teeth remain as good as ever. You never have to keep them in a glass on the bedside table.

Your whatchamacallits fall off, and you have to keep *them* in a glass on the bedside table, but nobody's perfect.

You can fly. Without a plane. Without uppers or Valium. Without air traffic controllers. Just *upsa-daisy!* and away you go. That's nice.

But the ultimate advantage to being a Real Extra-Terrestrial is this: you aren't to blame for any of what the citizens of Earth do to one another and to the planet. You're just an innocent bystander.

When it comes to monsters, nothing in creation is in a league with plain old Terrestrials.

That's the last joke in this book.

It's on us.

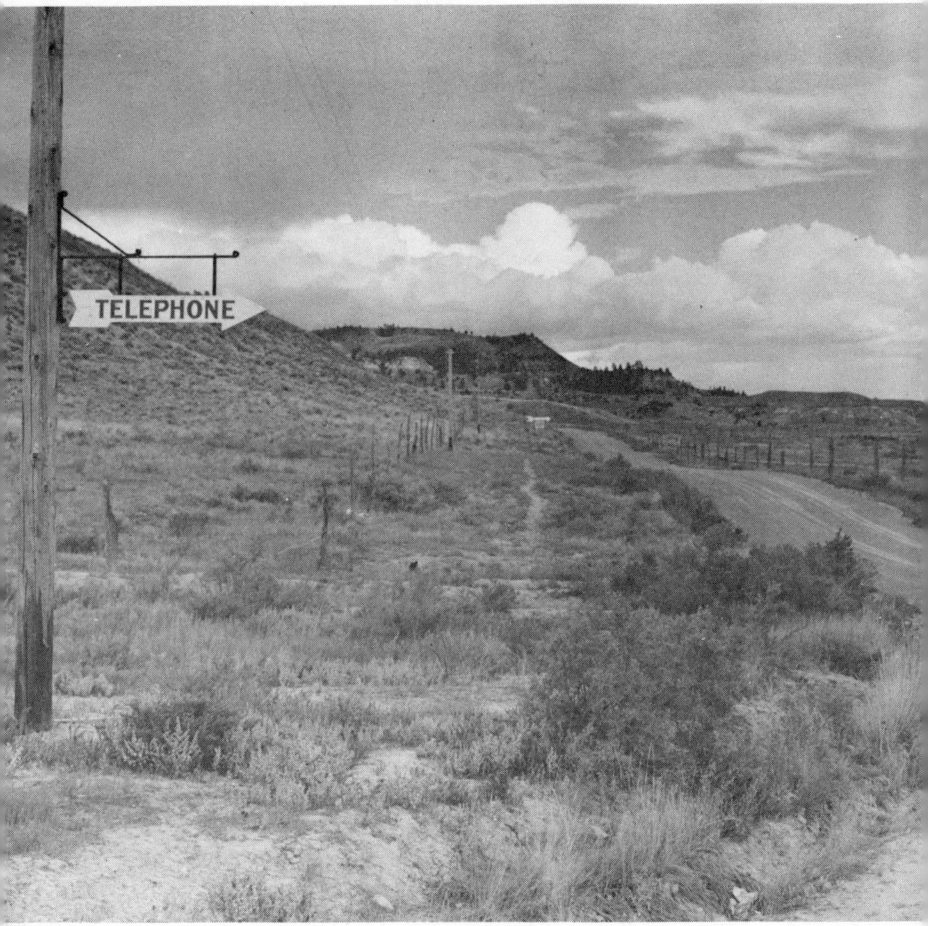
TELEPHONE